# Looking at

# Animals

## in

# COLD

# PLACES

First published in Great Britain in 1999 by

 **Belitha Press Limited,**
London House, Great Eastern Wharf,
Parkgate Road, London SW11 4NQ

This paperback edition first published in 2000

**Series Editor** Honor Head
**Series Designer** Hayley Cove
**Picture Researcher** Juliet Duff
**Map Artwork** Robin Carter / Wildlife Art Agency
**Animal Symbols** Arlene Adams

ISBN 1 84138 156 X (paperback)
ISBN 1 84138 018 0 (hardback)

Printed in China

10 9 8 7 6 5 4 3 2 1

British Library Cataloguing in Publication Data
for this book is available from the British Library

### Photographic credits
BBC Natural History Unit: 26 Jeff Foott. Biofotos: 27 Brian Rogers.
Bruce Coleman Ltd: 8 Johnny Johnson; 24 Jeff Foott; 28 Hans Reinhard.
Frank Lane Picture Agency: 6, 11 Silvestris; 16 Kurt Ramseyer;
23 Brake/Sunset; 29 M. Horning/Earthviews. Planet Earth Pictures:
13 Geoff du Feu; 14 Frank Krahmer; 19 Mark Mattock; 21 Tom Walker.
Oxford Scientific Films: 7 Doug Allan; 9 Dan Guravich; 10 Graham Wren; 12
E R Degginger; 15 Richard Farnell; 17, 22 Daniel Cox; 18 Michael Leach; 20
Tom Ulrich; 25 Zig Leszczynski.
### Cover
Bruce Coleman Ltd: top Hans Reinhard; bottom Johnny Johnson.
Planet Earth Pictures: centre right Frank Krahmer.

# Looking at
# Animals
## in
# COLD PLACES

Moira Butterfield

Belitha Press

# Introduction

The coldest places in the world are
in the far north and the far south.
The north is called the Arctic and the
south is called the Antarctic. These
are called polar places.

When it is winter in polar places there
are terrible storms and howling winds.
The sea is so cold it freezes over. Even
in summer polar places are very cold.

Some animals live in polar places all the
time. Some animals visit for the summer
only and leave in winter. All the animals
in polar places have their own special
ways of coping with the cold.

# Contents

# Harp seal

Seals live in cold places where it is snowy and icy. Harp seals live in the Arctic, the far north of the world. The babies have white fur. As they grow up, the white fur falls off, leaving a smooth skin. Seals are good at diving and swimming underwater so that they can catch fish to eat.

# Polar bear

Polar bears are big and strong, with sharp teeth and claws. They roam the frozen north looking for seals to eat. They can smell a seal from a long way off.

They have thick fur and fat to help keep them warm. The mother polar bear teaches her young to swim in the icy water.

# Lemming

Lemmings live in the Arctic. They stay out of the worst cold weather by hiding in underground burrows. Sometimes they pop outside to look for plants to eat. When they are outside they are in great danger because lots of other animals are hunting for them.

# Snowy owl

A snowy owl can swoop down to grab
a lemming in its sharp talons. The owl's
legs are covered in feathers right down
to its toes to help keep it warm.

The owl's white colour is a good
camouflage. The white feathers make
it hard to see the owl against the snow.

# Caribou

The caribou live in northern parts of the world in big groups called herds. They have thick coats to keep them warm. Their wide hoofs help them to walk in the snow.

Male caribou have giant antlers which they sometimes use to fight each other. Caribou are also called reindeer.

# Wolf

Wolves live with their families in groups called packs. They work together as a team of fast and fierce hunters. They chase and catch other animals such as caribou. Baby wolves learn to hunt by playing pretend fighting games with their brothers and sisters.

# Kittiwake

In spring kittiwakes and lots of other seabirds come north to the Arctic to lay their eggs. Thousands of the birds nest together in big, noisy crowds on cliff ledges.

They make their nests from moss and seaweed stuck together with droppings. They hatch two to three eggs.

# Musk ox

Musk oxen have shaggy, warm coats
so that they can stand freezing Arctic
snowstorms. They wander around in small
herds, looking for patches of moss and
grass to nibble. If wolves try to attack their
babies, the oxen stand in a circle with
the babies safely hidden in the middle.

# Arctic fox

In winter the Arctic fox has thick, white fur to camouflage it against the snow. In summer, when the snow melts, the fox's fur turns brown. Foxes can hear very well. When a fox hears a lemming rustling around it will creep up on it and then quickly pounce.

# Beluga whale

The beluga is a white whale that lives in the Arctic Ocean. It lives on tiny fish that it catches in its mouth as it swims along.

Whales have lots of fat called blubber underneath their skin. This keeps them warm when they swim in the freezing sea.

# Elephant seal

Elephant seals look big and fat because they have lots of blubber to keep them warm. When they are sitting on land they look clumsy, but when they are swimming in the sea they are very graceful. On land they call to each other by roaring loudly.

# Emperor penguin

Emperor penguins live in the Antarctic and like to leap in and out of the freezing sea. When a female lays an egg, a male carries it around in a fold of skin above his feet.

When the chick hatches it sits on the male's feet so that it doesn't touch the freezing ice.

# Where they live

This is a map of the world. It shows you where the animals live.

**ARCTI**

**NORTH AMERICA**

**SOUTH AMERIC**

☐ cold places

 harp seal

 polar bear

lemming

snowy owl

caribou

wolf

 kittiwake

musk ox

Arctic fox

beluga whale

elephant seal

emperor penguin

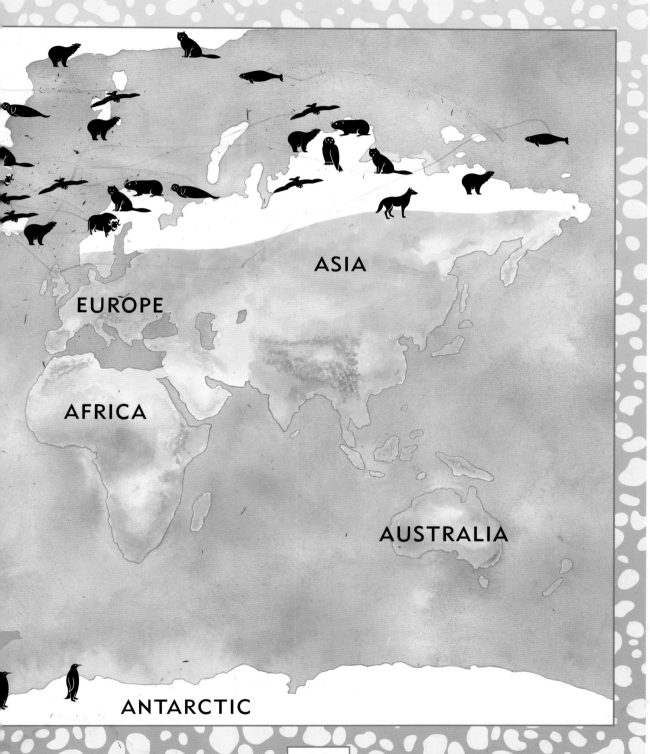

EUROPE

ASIA

AFRICA

AUSTRALIA

ANTARCTIC

# Index of words to learn